New Curriculum

Primary
Science
Learn, practise and revise

Year **5**

Alan Jarvis and
William Merrick

RISING STARS

Rising Stars UK Ltd, 7 Hatchers Mews, Bermondsey Street, London SE1 3GS

www.risingstars-uk.com

Every effort has been made to trace copyright holders and obtain their permission for the use of copyright materials. The authors and publisher will gladly receive information enabling them to rectify any error or omission in subsequent editions.

All facts are correct at the time of going to press.

Published 2013
Text, design and layout © Rising Stars UK Ltd.

Authors: Alan Jarvis and William Merrick
Science consultant: Shân Oswald, Improve Education
Text design: Green Desert Ltd
Cover design: West 8 Design
Illustrations: Oxford Designers and Illustrators; David Woodroffe
Publisher: Camilla Erskine
Editorial: Sparks (www.sparkspublishing.com)

British Library Cataloguing in Publication Data.
A CIP record for this book is available from the British Library.

ISBN: 978-0-85769-684-7

Printed by Craft Print International Ltd, Singapore

Contents

How to get the best out of this book

Each topic spreads across two pages and focuses on one major idea. Many of your lessons may be based on these topics. Each double page helps you to keep **On track** and **Aiming higher**.

Title and key ideas: tell you what you are aiming to learn. The second idea is always more difficult than the first.

Key information: sets out the key facts that you need to know and the ideas you need to understand fully.

Key questions: help you to learn more facts and understand the science in each topic. The investigations you do will give you the evidence you need to prove the scientific facts you've learnt.

Key words and their meanings: help build up your scientific vocabulary. Remember that some words mean one thing in everyday life and something more special in science.

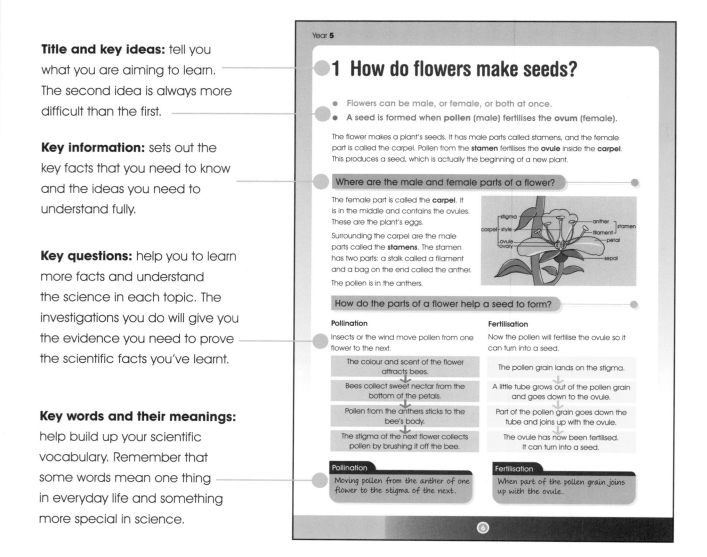

Follow these simple rules if you are using the book for revising.

1 Read each page carefully. Give yourself time to take in each idea.

2 Learn the key facts and ideas. Ask your teacher or mum, dad or the adult who looks after you if you need help.

3 Concentrate on the things you find more difficult.

4 Only work for about 20 minutes or so at a time. Take a break and then do more work.

The right-hand page has lots of fun questions for you to try. They help you to find how well you have understood what you have learned. There are questions on facts, ideas and scientific investigations. If you are stuck, the information on the left-hand page will help.

If you get most of the **On track** questions right then you are working at the expected level for the year. Well done – that's brilliant! If you get most of the **Aiming higher** questions right, you are working at the top of expectations for your year. You're doing really well!

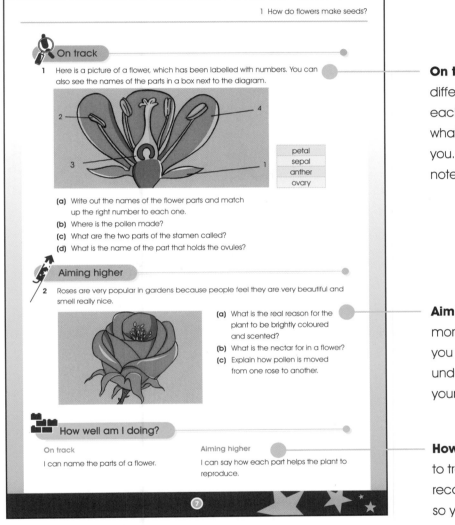

On track questions: come in different styles. Be sure to read each one carefully. Think about what the diagrams are telling you. Write your answers in your notebook.

Aiming higher questions: are more difficult. To answer them well, you have to know more facts or understand a harder idea. Write your answers in your notebook.

How well am I doing?: helps you to track progress. Keep a running record of how well you are doing so you keep on target.

Follow these simple rules if you want to know how well you are doing.

1 Work through the questions.

2 Check your answers with your teacher or using the answer booklet in the middle of the book.

3 Keep a record of how well you do.

4 Write down anything you are finding difficult and work through the chapter again to see if you can find the answer. If you are still finding it hard, ask your teacher for help.

1 How do flowers make seeds?

- Flowers can be male, or female, or both at once.
- **A seed is formed when pollen (male) fertilises the ovum (female).**

The flower makes a plant's seeds. It has male parts called stamens, and the female part is called the carpel. Pollen from the **stamen** fertilises the **ovule** inside the **carpel**. This produces a seed, which is actually the beginning of a new plant.

Where are the male and female parts of a flower?

The female part is called the **carpel**. It is in the middle and contains the ovules. These are the plant's eggs.

Surrounding the carpel are the male parts called the **stamens**. The stamen has two parts: a stalk called a filament and a bag on the end called the anther.

The pollen is in the anthers.

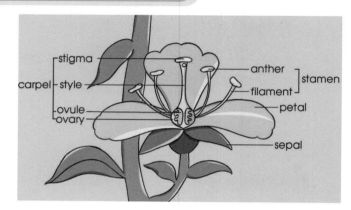

How do the parts of a flower help a seed to form?

Pollination

Insects or the wind move pollen from one flower to the next.

The colour and scent of the flower attracts bees.
Bees collect sweet nectar from the bottom of the petals.
Pollen from the anthers sticks to the bee's body.
The stigma of the next flower collects pollen by brushing it off the bee.

Fertilisation

Now the pollen will fertilise the ovule so it can turn into a seed.

The pollen grain lands on the stigma.
A little tube grows out of the pollen grain and goes down to the ovule.
Part of the pollen grain goes down the tube and joins up with the ovule.
The ovule has now been fertilised. It can turn into a seed.

Pollination

Moving pollen from the anther of one flower to the stigma of the next.

Fertilisation

When part of the pollen grain joins up with the ovule.

On track

1   Here is a picture of a flower, which has been labelled with numbers. You can also see the names of the parts in a box next to the diagram.

| petal |
| sepal |
| anther |
| ovary |

(a) Write out the names of the flower parts and match up the right number to each one.

(b) Where is the pollen made?

(c) What are the two parts of the stamen called?

(d) What is the name of the part that holds the ovules?

Aiming higher

2   Roses are very popular in gardens because people feel they are very beautiful and smell really nice.

(a) What is the real reason for the plant to be brightly coloured and scented?

(b) What is the nectar for in a flower?

(c) Explain how pollen is moved from one rose to another.

How well am I doing?

On track

I can name the parts of a flower.

Aiming higher

I can say how each part helps the plant to reproduce.

2 Do all plants reproduce in the same way?

- Flowering plants reproduce **sexually** when male and female parts make seeds.
- Some plants reproduce **asexually** when a small part splits off to grow on its own.

We use the word **reproduction** to talk about any way of making new plants and animals. The way flowers make seeds is called **sexual reproduction** because the male and female parts of the flower both give something towards making the seed. Some plants have different ways of reproducing that are not sexual.

What is the difference between sexual and asexual reproduction?

Sexual reproduction:

Male and **female** parts of the flower are involved.

The bee is bringing in pollen from the male **stamens** of one flower to the female **carpel** of another.

Asexual reproduction:

A **single** plant reproduces on its own without involving the flower.

The little plants on the ends of the long runners separate and live on their own. They are identical to their parents.

What difference do the two methods make?

Sexual reproduction brings **variety**.

There is a **range** of colours inherited from the parents. New types might appear that are better in some way.

Asexual reproduction means all of the new plants are **exactly the same** as the original parent. This could be a good thing or a bad thing.

The farmer has cut twigs from his best lavender plant. They grow into new plants. Now he can grow **identical copies** of the best plant. He could earn more money!

Sexual reproduction

Sexual reproduction needs two sexes of plants, male and female.

Asexual reproduction

Asexual means not sexual. Male and female plants are not needed.

On track

1

The bigger strawberry plant is sending out sideways **runners**.		Potatoes starting to sprout	
Cuttings from a cypress hedge have been planted.		A butterfly visits a flower for nectar.	

(a) Which are showing asexual reproduction?

(b) Which one is showing sexual reproduction?

Aiming higher

2 Leopard class grew a row of tomatoes in the school greenhouse. They measured how tall the plants grew.

(a) Where will the new seeds be found in these plants?

(b) What part of the plant grows into the tomato fruits?

(c) What was the smallest height?

(d) What was the most common height?

(e) What was the tallest plant?

(f) What is it about the heights that suggests the tomatoes were made by sexual reproduction?

Plant number	Plant height
1	100cm
2	90 cm
3	100 cm
4	110 cm
5	95 cm
6	100 cm
7	95 cm
8	105 cm
9	100 cm
10	105 cm

How well am I doing?

On track

I can describe the difference between sexual and asexual reproduction in plants.

Aiming higher

I can explain that sexual reproduction leads to variation in plants.

3 How do animals reproduce?

- All animals grow from eggs made inside a female.
- When an egg joins with a sperm from a male, it can grow into a new animal.

When a new animal is made there is always a male and a female. Even worms and insects have mums and dads! Some, like humans, look after their babies really well for many years, and insects don't look after theirs at all. Even so it always starts with two parents, one male and one female.

Do all animals have eggs?

All animals start from an **egg** which is made inside their mother.

- Birds and many other animals make large eggs which grow into babies **outside** the mother.
- Mammals' eggs are too small to see. They grow into babies **inside** the mother.

When a chicken lays an egg there is the beginning of a chick inside. About three weeks later it is ready to hatch.

We never see the sheep's egg. It stays inside the mother. She is **pregnant** for about 21 weeks until the lamb is born.

What makes the egg grow into a baby?

Mothers make eggs inside their bodies. Fathers make even smaller sperms inside theirs. The eggs and sperms have to join together. The sperm fertilises the egg so it can develop into a baby.

Fish lay their eggs straight into the water. The father adds tiny **sperms,** which swim to the eggs.

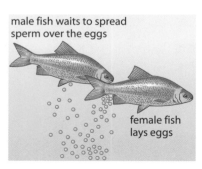

male fish waits to spread sperm over the eggs

female fish lays eggs

The father swan puts his sperm inside the mother, where they meet the eggs. The mother lays the eggs in her nest.

Reproduction
When animals or plants make new ones, it is called reproduction.

Fertilisation
When the sperm joins the egg so it can become a baby.

 **On track**

1 This is a scan of a baby growing inside the mother. Mothers have a scan while they are pregnant to make sure the baby is developing properly.

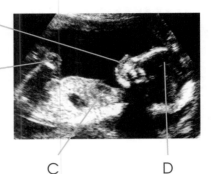

| mouth | foot | brain | heart |

(a) What are the names of the parts labelled A, B, C and D?

 Aiming higher

2 Leopard class knew that human women are pregnant for 9 months, which is about 270 days. That is how long it takes from the egg being fertilised until the baby is ready to be born.

They wondered how long it took for babies to grow inside other animal mothers, so Mr Hills found some facts out for them.

One person in the class thought that the **bigger** animals were pregnant for **longer.**

	Body mass	Length of pregnancy
Cat	4 kg	64 days
Chimp	50 kg	240 days
Human	70 kg	270 days
Sheep	80 kg	145 days
Deer	150 kg	200 days
Cow	800 kg	285 days
Elephant	4800 kg	616 days

(a) Do you think the figures show that it is true that bigger animals are pregnant for longer? Draw a graph to help you decide.

(b) Which animals do **not** quite fit that idea?

(c) A horse has a mass of 450 kilograms. How long do you think it would be pregnant for? Use your graph to find out.

 How well am I doing?

On track

I know that babies grow from eggs inside their mothers.

Aiming higher

I know that a father's sperm fertilises the egg so it can grow.

4 How do the life cycles of different animals vary?

- **Some baby animals are a lot like their parents.**
- **Some baby animals look completely different to their parents.**

An animal's life begins with a fertilised egg. Fertilised frogs eggs are found in a pond, where they turn into tadpoles. They don't look anything like frogs to start with – they become frogs later on. Mammals eggs grow inside the mother, and are born looking very much like the adult, only much smaller.

Which animals look similar to their babies?

Birds and mammals have life cycles where the babies are like their parents.

There is a difference. The bird's egg develops **outside** the mother. A mammal's egg develops **inside** the mother until the baby is ready to be born.

Birds

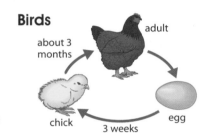

The chick changes its fluffy yellow feathers, but does not change much apart from that.

Mammals

There is a very tiny egg which becomes a puppy inside the mother. It looks like her when it is born.

Which animals change completely as they become adults?

Amphibians

Insects

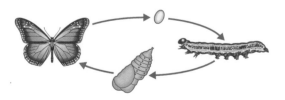

Big changes like this during development are called **metamorphosis.**

Development	Metamorphosis
The changes that take place in a creature as it grows.	A big change in the form of an animal as it grows and develops.

On track

1   Mammals, birds and reptiles do not have a metamorphosis, but they do change in some smaller ways. Copy out this chart of ways babies are different from their parents. See how many more things you can think of to add to it.

Baby bird

Cannot fly

Kitten

Eyes closed for the first few days

Only drink mother's milk

Aiming higher

2   Study this diagram of a fly's life cycle. Then use these words to fill in the missing words in the sentences below.

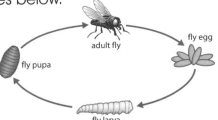

adult fly
fly egg
fly pupa
fly larva

larva	pupa
wings	eggs
metamorphosis	adult

(a) After the eggs hatch out the fly goes through two different stages before it becomes an _____.

(b) The first stage is normally called a maggot. Its scientific name is a _____.

(c) The second stage has a hard case round it. It is called a _____.

(d) Inside the pupa case the fly develops its _____.

(e) The adult starts off the whole life cycle again when it lays _____.

(f) A complete change like this is called a _____.

How well am I doing?

On track

I can describe some of the changes that reptiles, birds and mammals go through as they grow and develop.

Aiming higher

I can explain the changes that happen when an animal goes through a metamorphosis.

5 How do humans grow up?

- Boys and girls grow to their full sizes at different rates.
- As teenagers grow up their bodies change so they are ready to reproduce.

You are all busy growing up. You are growing taller and stronger, and learning more about the world. By the time you are 18 you will be full grown. Soon after that you might start a family of your own.

How do we change as we grow?

- **Infancy:** We are growing and learning control of our muscles so we can walk. As our brains develop we learn to talk.
- **Childhood:** Up to year six or seven we are counted as children, busy growing and learning, but still needing to be looked after by our parents.
- **Adolescence:** At secondary school we start to turn into adults. We reach full size and learn to look after ourselves and earn a living.
- **Adult:** At 18 we are adults. Adults are strong and know enough to work and care for their families
- **Old age:** When we get very old we may need to be cared for again.

How do people change as they get ready to have babies?

Special changes happen inside and outside our bodies as we start to get ready to have babies. People vary a lot, but it might take from age 10 to age 16.

Girls start to make their **eggs**, and boys begin to make the **sperms** that the eggs need to grow into babies.

Babies need a lot of looking after so people wait until they are properly grown up before starting their family.

We see other changes happening as well.

- Boys' voices 'break' which means they become deeper like a man's. Their beards start to grow as well.
- Girls' breasts grow so they can make milk when they have babies.

Puberty
The changes in our bodies that get use ready to make babies.

Adolescence
The years when we change from a child to an adult.

On track

1   Here are the stages of a human life cycle. Next to the picture you can see some statements about the different stages.

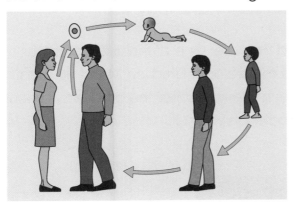

- Have to have everything done for them
- Are old enough to look after their own babies
- Are just turning into adults
- Can walk and talk but need looking after by their parents.

(a) Write out the names of four stages, and match each one up to the right statement.

(b) Which stage is often called 'teenager'?

(c) Make out a timeline chart showing the first 20 years of a person's life. Enter the stages of growing up onto it. The top part has been done for you.

Age	Stage	Main growing up events
0 years	Infancy	Baby is born
1 year	Infancy	
2 years		
3 years		

Aiming higher

2   A cat is an adult at one year old, but human beings are dependent on their parents for many years. Sally is 20 years old and her mum and dad still give her some money to help her at college.

(a) Why do humans stay dependent on their parents for such a long time?

(b) Name four things your parents do for you that help you survive and grow up.

How well am I doing?

On track

I can describe the main stages of a human's life cycle.

Aiming higher

I can explain why humans take much longer to grow up than other mammals.

6 Are some rocks harder than others?

- **Some rocks are hard and some are soft.**
- **You can do a scratch test to find out how hard they are.**

Rocks can be grouped according to how hard they are. One of the first scales was devised in 1812 by the German geologist and mineralogist Friedrich Mohs. His idea was that a hard material would scratch a softer material but not the other way around. You can use this idea to test the hardness of materials yourself.

What test were Leopard class asked to do?

Leopard class had some rocks to test. They had to find out which was the hardest and which was the softest.

They used four different objects to scratch each rock. They knew they had to press down on each rock exactly the same but found this difficult.

They put their results in a table.

What did they think about?

We each have a different rock to test. We will try to scratch them with the same force.

We are going to use a fingernail, coin, matchstick and plastic knife to scratch each rock. The hardest one will scratch most rocks.

We are going to measure whether the object scratches the rock or not.

Variable

A factor that we change, keep the same or measure when we are doing a test.

Table

A way of recording the results of a scientific test. It shows the variable you change and the one you measure.

On track

1   This table shows the results Leopard class obtained.

Rock	Was scratched by:			
	Fingernail	Coin	Matchstick	Plastic knife
Talc	Yes	Yes	Yes	Yes
Sandstone	No	Yes	No	Yes
Granite	No	No	No	No
Marble	No	Yes	No	Yes

(a)   They decided that granite was the hardest of the four rocks. Can you explain if you agree with their conclusion?

(b)   Copy the boxes out below. Write in your boxes the order of the rocks from hardest to softest.

Granite						

Hardest rock ← —————————————————— → Softest rock

(c)   Which of these statements explains why it was hard to keep the test fair?

The rocks were different sizes.	Each object had a different shape.
Some objects were harder than others.	It was hard to scratch the object with the same force.

Aiming higher

2   Mr Hills showed Leopard class the Mohs scale. The larger the number, the harder the rock. Use it to answer the following questions.

(a)   Explain why talc would **not** scratch any of the other rocks.

(b)   Name two rocks that quartz would scratch and one that it would not.

(c)   Glass is as hard as quartz. Would it scratch diamond? If not, explain why not.

1	Talc	6	Feldspar
2	Gypsum	7	Quartz
3	Calcite	8	Topaz
4	Flourite	9	Corundum
5	Apatite	10	Diamond

How well am I doing?

On track

I can describe how to test the hardness of rocks.

Aiming higher

I can explain how to carry out a fair test and why it might be hard to do.

7 How can magnets be used to group materials?

- You can easily test materials to see if they are magnetic.
- You can group materials according to if they are magnetic or not.

Leopard class were asked to group together all magnetic materials. They tried to narrow this down by testing out their hypotheses. First they started with a wide range of materials and then just those that were most likely to be magnetic.

Are only metals attracted to a magnet?

Jill and Ali investigated some materials to see if they were magnetic or not.

They tested an iron nail, a plastic spoon, a piece of chocolate, a steel paperclip and some matchsticks.

Only metals can be magnets

Metals and other materials can be magnets.

They used the same strong magnet every time. They brought it close to each material. They looked to see if the magnet attracted it.

Are all metals attracted to a magnet?

Jack and Efik tested just objects made out of metals.

They tested a gold ring, an iron nail, a steel paperclip, a brass washer, a silver spoon and a copper bracelet.

All metals are magnetic

Only a small number of metals are magnetic

They used a similar magnet to Jill and Ali. They too looked to see if their magnet attracted the metal or not. These are their results.

Attracted to a magnet		Not attracted to a magnet	
iron nail	steel paperclip	gold ring	brass washer
		silver spoon	copper bracelet

Hypothesis

A theory that would explain the facts.

Chart

A way of showing the results of a scientific test.

On track

1   Jill and Ali found out that the iron nail and the steel paperclip were the only materials that the magnet could pick up.

   (a) Draw a table to show their results more clearly.

   (b) Who had the better hypothesis?

   (c) Explain your answer.

Aiming higher

2   Jack and Efik tried to make sense of their results.

   (a) How many metals were attracted to their magnet and how many were not? Draw a bar chart to show this result.

   (b) What do these results show?

   (c) Who had the better hypothesis?

   (d) Explain your answer.

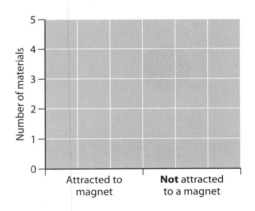

3   They tested some more metals. A nickel screw and a cobalt bar were attracted to a magnet but aluminium foil, a tin can, lead sheet and a zinc bar were not.

   (a) Draw a second bar chart that has the results from all the metals tested on it.

   (b) Who has the better hypothesis now?

   (c) What is the evidence now more reliable?

How well am I doing?

On track

I can describe how to test for magnetic materials.

Aiming higher

I can name four metals that are magnetic and eight that are not.

8 What materials will let electricity flow?

- **Electric conductors** allow electricity to flow easily through them.
- **Electrical insulators** do not allow electricity to flow through them.

Electrical conductors and insulators are two **groups** of materials. Electrical circuits will only work if the electricity can flow all the way around.

What materials could you test?

Leopard class tested some materials in a circuit to see if they conducted electricity or not.

metal coin

iron nail

plastic ruler

paperclip

silver spoon

What results did Leopard class get?

Four out of the five objects and materials that they tested conducted electricity. The materials need to be electrical insulators for this to happen.

Name of material	Steel paperclip	Metal coin	Iron Nail	Plastic ruler	Silver spoon
Does it conduct electricity?	Yes	Yes	Yes	No	Yes

They made a simple circuit but it had a gap in it. Their idea was to let the clips hold the materials one by one. This would make sure the gap was filled.

If a material conducts electricity, the circuit would be complete and a current could flow.

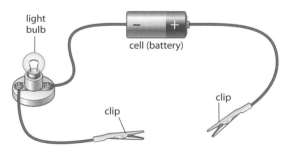

They would know this because the bulb would glow bright.

If it didn't conduct electricity, no current would flow and the bulb would stay unlit.

Stephen Gray

Discovered that some materials could carry electricity.

Graphene

A modern material that is not a metal but conducts electricity very well.

On track

1   Think carefully about Leopard class's tests on electrical conductors.

What was kept the same	What was changed	What was observed changing

(a) Make a table like this one. Fill it in using the details of how they did their test.

(b) Explain how they knew if a material was an electrical conductor or insulator.

(c) Which one of these was presented in their table?

plans	predictions	ideas	questions	results	theories

2   One group draw a bar chart of their results. They say the table is better than the bar chart. Look carefully at the bar chart and the table.

(a) What extra information does the table give?

(b) What kind of material does the table show always conducts electricity?

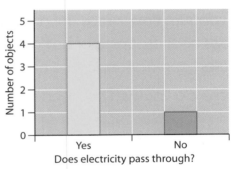

Aiming higher

3   Mr Hills gave them an extra challenge. He wanted Leopard class to come up with a big list of electrical conductors and electrical insulators. He reminded them of the rule that 'Metals conduct electricity'. Here are some materials to start you thinking.

wood	aluminium foil	glass	cotton	gold

(a) Sort these five materials into electrical conductors or insulators.

(b) Sort the other materials on these pages and add them to your group.

(c) Add five other materials to each group.

(d) What group would graphene belong to?

How well am I doing?

On track

I can explain how to test a material to show if it conducts electricity or not.

Aiming higher

I can group materials into electrical conductors and insulators.

9 What is the best heat insulator to use?

- Heat insulators can keep things hot or cold.
- Materials that are NOT metals are usually good heat insulators.

Your clothes keep you warm. They are made out of materials that are good heat insulators. They keep the heat in and don't let it escape. Heat insulators can also keep things cold, which could seem strange! This is useful on hot summer days.

Heat insulators and conductors are two **groups** of materials.

What can you use to keep things hot or cold?

A **vacuum flask** keeps hot drinks warm. Its special design stops heat escaping or going into the flask. Inside, a double-walled container holds the hot liquid.

There is a vacuum between the walls which means there is nothing there, not even air. The rest of the flask is mostly made of plastic and glass.

It works because heat cannot travel through the vacuum. A vacuum is even better at insulating than air. The glass and plastic are both good heat insulators.

The flask can also keep things cold inside. The insulating design and materials stop heat going in and warming up the cold contents.

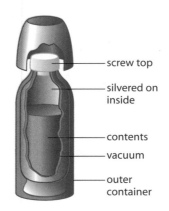

screw top

silvered on inside

contents

vacuum

outer container

The flask is made of insulating materials. It design also includes a vacuum, which means a space with nothing inside it.

What materials are good heat insulators?

Materials can be grouped into good and poor heat insulators. You can devise a fair test to see which of these groups a material fits into.

Good heat insulators			Poor heat insulators		
wool	air	plastic	iron	copper	aluminium
wood	rubber	paper			

Vacuum flask

Reinhold Berger and Albert Aschenbrenner invented the vacuum flask in 1907.

Heat insulator

A material that stops heat moving in either direction.

On track

1   Mr Hills gave Leopard class some tubs of ice cream and some bags made out of different materials. He asked them to plan an investigation to find out which bag is best at stopping the ice cream from melting.

(a) Which of these pieces of apparatus would they need to do their investigation?

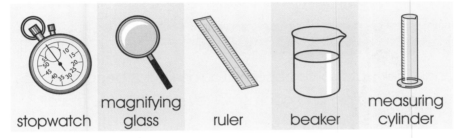

stopwatch   magnifying glass   ruler   beaker   measuring cylinder

(b) Write out these sentences. Choose the best word in **bold** to explain the idea behind the investigation.

The best bag will **conduct/insulate** well.

It will stop **cold/heat** passing from the air to the ice cream.

(c) Make a table that shows what variables they should keep the same, change and measure in their investigation.

Aiming higher

2   Mr Hills brought in his food box. He asked the class what he could do with it to keep his cold drink cold. What else could he use besides his cold box?

(a) List several ways his class could keep the drinks cold.

(b) Describe how they might test their ideas?

(c) Explain what they would record.

(d) How will they know which method is best?

How well am I doing?

On track

I can name some materials that are good heat insulators.

Aiming higher

I can plan a test that shows which material is the best heat insulator.

10 Can some changes be reversed?

- Mixing materials can be reversed in other ways.
- Heating and cooling reverse changes of state.

Materials are usually found as solids, liquids or gases. These are called the three states of matter. It can be useful to change a material from one state to another. Changes of state can always be reversed by heating or cooling. Some mixtures can be separated by magnets, evaporation or filtering.

How can changes of state be reversed?

When materials change their state solids become liquids, liquids become gases or solids and gases become liquids. Heating and cooling will reverse changes of state.

The boiling kettle changes liquid water into water vapour. The cold window  changes it back into liquid water again.

Scientists give names to changes of state. Liquid to gas is **evaporation**. Gas to liquid is **condensation**.

Heating solid chocolate makes it melt into a liquid. Letting it cool changes it back into a solid again.

Liquid to solid is **freezing** or **solidifying**. Solid to liquid is **melting**.

How else can changes be reversed?

Sand and water have been mixed. A magnet will reverse the change. It will lift out the iron filings, leaving the sand behind.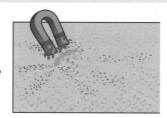

Salt has been added to the water. The salt can be dissolved. If you leave it, the water slowly evaporates and leaves the salt crystals behind.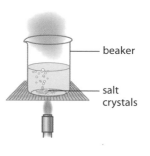

beaker

salt crystals

Reversible
Capable of being changed back into its original state.

State of matter
Describes if a material is a solid, liquid or gas.

On track

1   Leopard class were asked to think about these four pictures. They each show a change. Each could be easily changed and then changed back.

butter melting on toast

water freezing into ice

steel nails and brass screws mixed up

solid wax melting into liquid wax

(a) Draw out the table below. Fill it in.

What has happened?	How can it be reversed?
Butter has melted on toast.	
The liquid water is freezing solid.	
The steel nails and brass screws have been mixed together.	
The solid wax is melting.	

Aiming higher

2   Sam has mixed up some salt and sand. He wants to get them both back again and reverse the change. He adds water to the mixture.

(a) How could he separate the sand from the salty water?

(b) What would he then do to get the salt back?

How well am I doing?

On track

I can describe how changes of state can be reversed.

Aiming higher

I can describe a wider range of reversible changes.

11 What changes are irreversible?

- Some changes result in new materials being formed.
- These changes are not usually reversible.

When heat causes a material to change its state, the change can easily be reversed. But heating can also make new materials. Once done, it is nearly always impossible to get the original materials back. The change is **irreversible**. Burning and rusting are good examples of irreversible changes.

What can happen when you heat materials?

Heating chocolate makes it melt from a solid into a liquid. If you let it cool down, it turns back into a solid. This is a **reversible** change.

Heating an egg is very different. The eggs change completely. You cannot get the raw egg back. New materials have been made. The change is **irreversible**.

Can burning and rusting be reversed?

When wood burns in the air, smoke and ash are made. You cannot get the wood back again. The change is irreversible. Wood will not burn without air and heat to start the reaction.

The iron in this old car has rusted. Oxygen and water have made a new material with the iron. The iron has been oxidised. The change is irreversible.

Irreversible

A change that cannot easily be reversed to get back the materials you started with.

Oxidised

A material that has combined with oxygen from the air to make a new material.

On track

1 Changes happen when the candle is lit. Some wax melts and some burns.

(a) Are the changes reversible? Copy the table.
Write yes or no in the second column.

Change	Is the change reversible?
The wax melts.	
The wax burns.	

(b) Which of these statements are true or false? Copy and complete the table.

Statement	True	False
The wax must be heated to melt.		
Burning is a reversible change.		
When a solid melts it changes into a gas.		
Some of the new materials made escape into the air.		

Aiming higher

2 Mr Hills holds some materials over a candle flame.

(a) Describe one thing he has done to make the experiment safe.

(b) Wood and bread burn in the flame.
Are these changes reversible?
How do you know?

(c) Which of these materials will burn in a candle flame? Which ONE will rust?

cardboard	iron nail	plastic cup	steel spoon	cotton wool
matchstick	pound coin	stone	kitchen foil	gold ring

How well am I doing?

On track

I can explain what an irreversible change is.

Aiming higher

I can name some examples of irreversible changes.

12 What changes can sieves and filter papers reverse?

- Sieves can separate mixtures of solids with different sized particles.
- Filter papers can separate solid particles from water.

If you mingle two or more solids together you make a mixture. Sometimes you can see the different solids because they are different sizes or colours. Adding a solid to a liquid also makes a mixture. Sometimes the solid doesn't dissolve and it is easy to see. Often you can **reverse the change** by using sieves or filter papers. Magnets can help separate out magnetic materials like iron filings and steel paper clips.

How do you sieve a mixture of more than one solid?

Leopard class discussed how to separate a mixture of sand, rice and dried peas.

'The mixture has different sized particles. The peas are much larger than the other two. Rice grains are bigger than sand.'

'Let's use the sieve with the big holes first and then the other one.'

'Look what happens! The big peas cannot get through the sieve with the big holes but rice and sand can.'

The sieve with the smaller holes lets the sand through to the bowl but traps the rice. The mixture has separated!

How can you clean up dirty water?

Leopard class then discussed how to separate a mixture of sand and water.

'The smallest sieve we have still lets both the sand and water go through. We need an even finer sieve.'

'Filter paper is like a fine sieve. It looks solid, but when you look at it with a microscope you can see it isn't.'

Mixture
A substance that contains two or more materials that can be separated.

Filter paper
A special piece of paper with fine holes used for separating a liquid from a solid.

On track

1   This container has sand and stones mixed up with water.

   (a) What would happen if you passed the mixture through
        a sieve with large holes?

   (b) Describe what you might do then to make sure you
        had separated all three materials.

Aiming higher

2   Mr Hills gave his class a mixture of iron filings,
    sand, gravel and paper clips. He asked
    them to devise a way of separating them
    from each other.

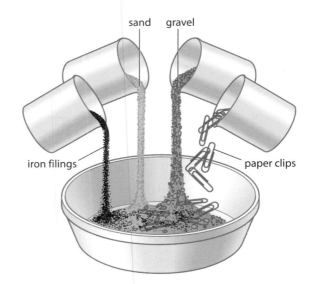

sand   gravel

iron filings   paper clips

   (a) Describe how they might separate
        the mixture.

   (b) What equipment would they use?

   (c) In what order would they do their
        separation?

3   Explain how you would separate a mixture of rice,
    pasta, salt and water.

How well am I doing?

On track

I can explain how a sieve separates some
mixtures of solids.

Aiming higher

I can explain when a filter paper or magnet
might be used to separate a mixture.

13 How well does sugar dissolve?

- Fair tests help you investigate dissolving.
- Sometime errors can creep in but you can spot these.

Mr Hills has told his class that sugar dissolves in water. Their job is to find out how the temperature of the water affects the time it takes for the sugar to dissolve. They had to plan, carry out and make sense of their investigation. Harry predicted, 'The sugar will dissolve more quickly when the water is hotter.'

How did Leopard class plan their test?

To make their test fair they used 20g of sugar and 200cm³ of water in every test.

They used hot water from the kettle and added cold water to it until the temperature was 30°C, then added the sugar and stirred it gently.

They timed how long it took the sugar to dissolve. They made sure the water stayed at 30°C using a nightlight. They did this three times.

Another group did exactly the same but the temperature of the water was 40°C.

Two other groups used water at 50°C and 60°C. The class shared all their results.

Were there any errors in their results?

Different groups did the test. The more readings they took, the more reliable the results, because any errors could be spotted. These are their results.

Temperature of water (°C)	Time (minutes)		
	Test 1	Test 2	Test 3
30	11	9	11
40	8	8	10
50	**11**	9	7
60	6	7	6

If you look at their first test, you can see the time at 50°C looks odd. It is higher than the one at 40°C. This does not seem to fit the pattern. There may be more than one!

Anomalous (odd) result
A result that does not seem to fit a pattern.

Error
A mistake.

On track

1   Mr Hills quizzed his class about how they planned and did their investigation.

(a) Which of these following pieces of apparatus did they use?

scales	beaker	filter	stirring rod	spoon	magnet
measuring cylinder	test tube	switch	sieve	kettle	thermometer

(b) Name the **one** factor they changed as they carried out their investigation.

(c) Name the factors they kept the same to make their investigation fair.

(d) Someone said that doing the test three times made it fair. Is this true?

(e) Mr Hills spotted Harry and Sara measuring the temperature of the water in different ways.
Which one is doing it correctly? Explain your answer.

Aiming higher

2   Mr Hills asked them some questions about their results. Can you answer them?

(a) Which results in the table are 'odd' ? Explain why they might have occurred.

(b) Do the three tests show a pattern? If so, explain what it is.

(c) Does the evidence in the table support Harry's prediction? Explain your answer.

(d) Some children gave the following reasons to explain why their test was fair.
Which do you think is the best explanation and why?

- We all had a turn at stirring the solution.
- We did a fair test because we kept everything the same.
- We did each temperature three times and found the average.
- Some water stayed in the measuring cylinder.

How well am I doing?

On track

I can plan a fair test.

Aiming higher

I can spot errors in a results table and explain why they might occur.

14 How can you get sugar back once it has dissolved?

- Solids can be recovered once they have dissolved in water. It can be reversed.

- Dissolving is when a solid mixes with a liquid so that you can't see the solid anymore.

If you put some sugar crystals into water, they will dissolve. The two things have made a special mixture called a solution. It looks like the sugar has disappeared, but you know it hasn't because the water tastes sweet. Mr Hills wanted his class to think about how they might reverse this change and get the sugar back. They could choose any equipment they liked to test out their ideas.

Can you get the sugar back by filtering?

Natalya and Ali decided to pass the sugary water through a filter paper.

Natalya said, 'I think the sugar will be left on the paper.'

Ali said, I think nothing will be left and everything will go into the beaker.'

They found out that everything passed through into the beaker. Ali was right.

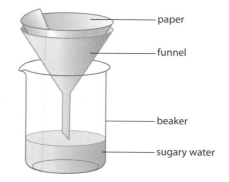

paper

funnel

beaker

sugary water

Can you get the sugar back by evaporating?

Sara and Haroun tried another way.

They decided to put the sugary water into a small bowl and leave it on a warm radiator for a couple of hours.

They found out that most of the water evaporated into the air. Sugar crystals were left behind in the bowl.

When they left it longer, only sugar was left. The water had changed state and evaporated into the air.

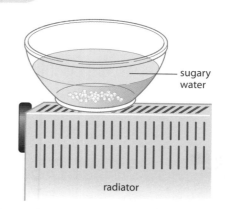

sugary water

radiator

Observation	Fact
Something you see happening.	An observation that has been confirmed repeatedly.

Unit		On track		Aiming higher
1 How do flowers make seeds?	**1 (a)** **(b)** **(c)** **(d)**	1 sepal 2 anther 3 ovary 4 petal In the anthers on the end of the stamens. Anther and filament Ovary	**2 (a)** **(b)** **(c)**	To attract insects to pollinate the flower. Nectar attracts pollinating insects. Pollen rubs off the anthers on to the bee while it is collecting nectar, and then on to the stigma of the next flower it visits.
2 Do all plants reproduce in the same way?	**1 (a)** **(b)**	Strawberry plant, cypress cuttings, sprouting potatoes. Flower being pollinated.	**2 (a)** **(b)** **(c)** **(d)** **(e)** **(f)**	Inside the tomatoes The flower becomes the fruit 90 cm 100 cm Plant 4 The variation in height
3 How do animals reproduce?	**1 (a)**	A – mouth B – foot C – heart D – brain	**2 (a)** **(b)** **(c)**	Generally bigger animals are pregnant for longer. The chimp and human are pregnant for longer than their mass would suggest. Roughly 250 days.
4 How do the life cycles of different animals vary?	**1**	Baby birds: need to be fed by parents, have no feathers, eyes closed for the first few days Kittens: only drink mother's milk, cannot stand or walk to start with.	**2 (a)** **(b)** **(c)** **(d)** **(e)** **(f)**	adult larva pupa wings eggs metamorphosis
5 How do humans grow up?	**1 (a)** **(b)** **(c)**	Baby – Have to have everything done for them. Children – Can walk and talk but need looking after by their parents. Adolescent – Are just turning into adults. Adults – Are old enough to look after their own babies. Adolescent A suitable timeline	**2 (a)** **(b)**	Humans grow slowly and there is much to learn. Suitable answers include: provide food/clothing/a home/education/protection
6 Are some rocks harder than others?	**1 (a)** **(b)** **(c)**	Granite is hardest because none of the test objects could scratch it. Granite, Marble, Sandstone, Talc The most difficult one to control is scratching each one with the same force.	**2 (a)** **(b)** **(c)**	Talc is softer than the other rocks. <table><tr><th>Quartz would scratch:</th><th>Quartz would not scratch:</th></tr><tr><td>Talc</td><td>Topaz</td></tr><tr><td>Gypsum</td><td>Corundum</td></tr><tr><td>Calcite</td><td>Diamond</td></tr><tr><td>Flourite</td><td></td></tr><tr><td>Apatite</td><td></td></tr><tr><td>Feldspar</td><td></td></tr></table>No, because diamond is harder than both.

Unit		On track		Aiming higher
7 How can magnets be used to group materials?	**1 (a)**	<table><tr><td>Material</td><td>Attracted to magnet?</td></tr><tr><td>iron nail</td><td>yes</td></tr><tr><td>plastic spoon</td><td>no</td></tr><tr><td>chocolate</td><td>no</td></tr><tr><td>steel paperclip</td><td>yes</td></tr><tr><td>matchstick</td><td>no</td></tr></table>	**2 (a)** **(b)** **(c)** **(d)** **3 (a)** **(b)** **(c)**	Two metals were attracted to the magnet and four were not. The results show that not many metals are magnetic. Most are not. Nina *Own answers* A suitable graph Nina. The evidence is more reliable because a wider range of metals has been tested.
	(b) **(c)**	Ali *Own answers*		
8 What materials will let electricity flow?	**1 (a)** **(b)** **(c)** **2 (a)** **(b)**	What was kept the same: Bulb, cell, wires, clips What was changed: Material being tested What was observed changing: Whether the bulb lit up or not. If the bulb lit the material was a conductor. Results The table tells which particular metals are conductors and non-conductors. Metals	**3 (a)** **(b)** **(c)** **(d)**	Aluminium and gold conduct electricity; the others do not. Steel, iron, silver. *Own answers* Electrical conductor
9 What is the best heat insulator to use?	**1 (a)** **(b)** **(c)**	Stopwatch The best bag will **insulate** well. It will stop **heat** passing from the air to the ice cream. Keep the same: Temperature of ice cream to start with, Same sized tub of ice-cream, room temperature. Change: Type of bag Measure: Time taken for ice cream to melt.	**2 (a)** **(b)** **(c)** **(d)**	Put them in a fridge/wrap them in ice; keeping them in a bucket of water; keep them in the shade/in the breeze. Always have a comparison – one in the shade, one in the sun, for example. Measure temperature at start and then in 10 minute intervals. An hour would be long enough. Changing temperature. The one where the temperature rises most slowly.
10 Can some changes be reversed?	**1 (a)**	<table><tr><td>What has happened?</td><td>How can it be reversed?</td></tr><tr><td>Butter melting</td><td>Allow it to cool down</td></tr><tr><td>Liquid water freezing</td><td>Warm it up</td></tr><tr><td>Steel and brass mixture</td><td>Remove nails with magnet</td></tr><tr><td>Solid wax melting</td><td>Cool it down</td></tr></table>	**2 (a)** **(b)**	He can filter out the sand with a filter paper. Boil the salty water so the water evaporates, leaving the salt behind.
11 What changes are irreversible?	**1 (a)** **(b)**	The wax melts – Yes The wax burns – No The wax must be heated to melt – True Burning is a reversible change – False When a solid melts it changes into a gas – False Some of the new materials made escape into the air – True	**2 (a)** **(b)** **(c)**	He is holding the burning material with tongs. Not reversible. Materials are escaping. Burn in a candle flame – cardboard, plastic cup, cotton wool, and matchstick. Rust – iron nail

On track

1   Mr Hills quizzed the class. He wrote four statements about the filtering method.

- The solid disappears when it dissolves.
- The solid melts into the water when it dissolves.
- The sugar solution is heavier than the water.
- Evaporation makes the water disappear.

(a) Only one of these statements is true. Which one?

(b) Pick one of the false statements and explain how you could you show your friends why it is wrong.

2   Explain why both the sugar and water go through the filter paper.

Aiming higher

3   Mr Hills asked the class some questions about the second test.

(a) What observation made it clear to Sara and Haroun that their method had worked?

(b) Why did they have to wait a couple of hours?

(c) Is adding sugar to water a reversible change?

(d) What name would you give to this method? Use a sentence like 'Separating by _____'

4   Which of these mixtures could you separate by this method?

- Rice, sand, peas and stones
- Sand and water
- Sand and iron nails
- Salty water

How well am I doing?

On track

I can explain the difference between dissolving, filtering and evaporation.

Aiming higher

I can name some mixtures that might be separated by evaporation.

15 What makes a material useful?

- Materials have many different properties.
- The properties help decide which material is best for a particular job.

Materials have many different properties. Some properties are useful for particular jobs and others are not. Scientists use the word 'material' to mean all the substances things are made from – which is everything in the Universe. If you know the properties of a material, you can decide what to use it for.

What properties are important?

Different materials can be used for the same job if they have a property in common. The properties of some materials make them useful for many different things.

Jumpers can be made from man-made or natural materials because they are good heat insulators.

Buckets are made from plastic or metal because both materials are light and strong.

Windows and bottles are made from glass because it is transparent and hard.

How can you make up your mind what material to use?

Materials don't have just one property. You need to consider more than property when deciding to use a material for a particular job. No material is perfect!

Material	Property					
	Transparent	Hard	Flexible	Conducts electricity	Waterproof	Brittle
Wood	No	Yes	No	No	Yes	No
Glass	Yes	Yes	No	No	Yes	Sometimes
Ceramic	No	Yes	No	No	Sometimes	Yes
Rubber	No	Yes	Yes	No	Yes	No
Iron	No	Yes	No	Yes	Yes	No
Plastic	Sometimes	Sometimes	Sometimes	No	Yes	No

Synthetic material

A material made by chemical reactions in the laboratory.

Ceramic

Baked clay. Tiles and flower pots are made of ceramic materials.

On track

1   Mr Hills has written out some science vocabulary for his class. Some are the names of materials and some are properties.

concrete	transparent	strong	ceramic
hard	wool	plastic	flexible

(a) Sort the words into two lists.

Names of materials	Properties of materials

Aiming higher

2   Mr Hills asked the class to complete the following sentences. For each material give **two** properties that make it good for its job.

(a) Iron is used to build bridges because _____

(b) Rubber is used for wellington boots because _____

(c) Leather is used for shoes because _____

(d) Stone is used for pavements because _____

(e) Cardboard is used for boxes because _____

(f) Electrical plugs are made from plastic because _____.

3   Make up similar sentences of your own for five new materials and the jobs they are best at.

How well am I doing?

On track

I can name some properties that make a material useful.

Aiming higher

I can decide and explain what makes a material good for a particular job.

16 Can mixing materials change them?

- Mixing some materials can produce new materials.
- Your observations will tell you if something new has been made.

How can you spot if new materials are being formed? There are many signs! A changing colour, a new smell, bubbles and substances getting warm all show that a chemical change is taking place. These changes are not usually reversible.

What can water do when mixed with some materials?

Mixing materials with water sometimes produces irreversible or chemical changes. This means that you cannot get back what you started with.

A hard solid is made from cement powder and water. This change is irreversible.

Plaster of Paris and water also make a hard solid. This change is reversible.

What can acids do when they are mixed with some materials?

Mixing some materials with an acid, such as vinegar or lemon juice, can also produce irreversible changes.

Mixing lemon juice with washing soda produces bubbles or carbon dioxide. This is one of the new materials made. You cannot get the original materials back.

Chemical change

A process in which materials react and form new substances.

Acids

Materials with a sour taste that react with some others to form carbon dioxide gas.

On track

1 Leopard class have mixed some materials together. Their observations are in this table. However, they have been mixed up.

What is mixed	Observation
plaster of paris and water	bubbles of gas come off.
vinegar and water	a hard, grey solid is formed.
cement and water	they just mix.
orange juice and washing soda	a hard, white solid is formed.

(a) Copy the table out. Match the correct observation to the mixture by drawing a straight line between them.

(b) Which ones are irreversible changes? How did you decide?

Aiming higher

2 Mr Hills shows his class a bottle with a balloon attached. Inside the bottle is some vinegar. He adds the bicarbonate of soda in the balloon to the vinegar. The balloon inflates. He shows them a graph. This displays how much the balloon inflates when different liquids are added. Use it to answer the questions.

Before adding bicarbonate of soda

balloon with bicarbonate of soda

vinegar

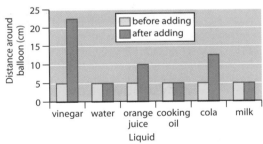

(a) Which three liquids reacted to produce a gas. How would you know there was a reaction?

(b) What do you think the three liquids chosen in part **a** have in common?

(c) Describe how the height of the bars on the chart shows which balloons inflate.

How well am I doing?

On track

I can explain what a chemical change is.

Aiming higher

I can explain some signs of chemical changes.

17 What new materials have chemists made?

- Chemical reactions can make useful new materials.
- **Many new materials have had or could have a big impact on our lives.**

One hundred years or so ago we had to use materials that were only found in nature. Imagine a life without plastics, modern medicines, artificial fibres and alloys. In the 20th century there was an explosion in the number of new materials that were invented. New materials with unique properties are still being made today.

How can chemists change our everyday lives?

Spencer Silver (1968): One of the inventors of low-tack adhesive. This allows notes to be easily attached and removed without leaving marks or residue.

Ruth Benerito (1950s): Invented wrinkle-free cotton. Clothes made out of this material could be 'washed and worn'. This changed the fabric industry and made cotton a very desirable fabric.

What new materials have been invented recently?

Harry Kroto (1985): One of the inventors of Buckminsterfullerene. This has a unique arrangement of 60 carbon atoms. It helps treat cancer.

Kostya Novoselov and Andre Geim (2003): Discovered graphene. Carbon atoms are arranged in layers, one atom thick. It is an amazing electrical conductor.

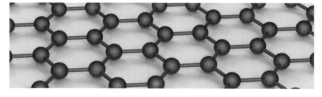

Chemist

A scientist who makes new materials out of the elements.

Alloys

Mixtures of metals that have better properties than the metals they are made from.

On track

1   Use the Internet to find out which of these materials occur naturally and which have been made by chemists.

cement	superglue	gold	plaster of Paris	polythene
diamond	graphene	wrinkle-free cotton	granite	low-tack adhesives

Aiming higher

2   Leopard class have done some research on chemicals that have changed our lives.

Material	Discoverer/inventor	Significance
Aspirin	Felix Hoffman (1897)	Used as a pain killer and for the treatment of heart disease
Bakelite	Leo Hendrik Baekeland (1907)	One of the first plastics
Penicillin	Alexander Fleming (1928)	A widely used antibiotic
Nylon	Wallace Carothers (1935)	One of the most commercially successful plastics
Halothane	Charles Sucking (1951)	A widely used general anaesthetic
Aspartame	Monsanto Chemicals (1965)	The most widely used artificial sweetener

(a) Draw a timeline showing the development of these new materials and their uses.

(b) Use the Internet to add a few more, from the past and modern times.

How well am I doing?

On track

I can name some famous chemists and the materials they invented.

Aiming higher

I can name some new materials that have had a big impact on everyday life.

18 What is in the solar system?

- **The Sun is at the centre of our solar system.**
- **Eight large planets and at least one dwarf planet orbit the Sun.**

We now know that the solar system contains eight planets. Galileo knew about six of these, including the Earth, because he had seen them through his telescope. Since then two more large planets have been found. William Herschel, an English astronomer, discovered Uranus in 1781. Johann Galle, from Germany, discovered Neptune in 1846.

What is at the centre of our solar system?

The Sun is just a star! It is very big compared with the Earth. It has a diameter of about 1,391,000 km and is 149,600,000 km away from the Earth. It looks different from other stars in the sky because it is much closer to Earth.

The Sun is a huge sphere of gas. Non-stop nuclear reactions take place in this star, changing hydrogen gas into helium gas. They release huge amounts of energy.

Inside the Sun the temperature is about 14 million degrees.

What are the names of the eight planets?

Eight large planets orbit our Sun. In order of distance from the Sun, they are: Mercury, Venus, Earth, Mars, Jupiter, Saturn, Uranus and Neptune.

Pluto, which is much smaller, was once grouped with the planets. It is very small and called a dwarf planet. Other dwarf planets have also been found.

Orbit

The path of a planet around the Sun.

Mnemonic

A sentence that helps you remember an idea or a set of facts.

On track

1. Mr Hills gave Leopard class a table of data about the eight planets. He had put the planets in alphabetical order.

Planet	Distance from the Sun (km)	Diameter (km)	Time it takes to orbit the Sun (Earth days or years)
Earth	149,600,000	12,756	365.25 days
Jupiter	778,369,000	142,984	11.86 years
Mars	227,936,640	6,794	687 days
Mercury	57,900,000	4,878	88 days
Neptune	4,496,976,000	49,532	164.8 years
Saturn	1,427,034,000	120,536	29 years
Uranus	2,870,658,186	51,118	84 years
Venus	108,160,000	12,104	243 days

(a) Make table. Put the eight planets in order of their distance from the Sun.

(b) Make a second table. This time order the planets in terms of their size.

(c) Can you see any pattern in the data? If so, explain what it is.

Aiming higher

2. Leopard class enjoyed making a model of our solar system.

(a) Make a drawing of their solar system looking down from above.

(b) Label the names of the planets.

(c) Explain the difference between a planet and a star.

(d) Write a mnemonic to help the class remember the names of the eight large planets.

How well am I doing?

On track

I can explain what makes the sun so hot and bright.

Aiming higher

I can name all the planets in our solar system.

19 How does the Earth move?

- The Earth moves once around the Sun in a roughly circular orbit once a year.

- The Earth's year is not exactly 365 days.

Why is a year almost always 365 days? The answer is to do with the way the Earth orbits the Sun. Your next birthday will come around when the Earth gets back to where it started on your last birthday. Even though the Earth travels a long way, and at a fast speed, the length of a year remains the same. Isn't that amazing?

What does the Earth's orbit look like?

The Earth's orbit is nearly circular, with the Sun at the centre. Looking from above, it moves anticlockwise around the Sun. The Earth's axis is tilted as well. It spins on its axis once every day.

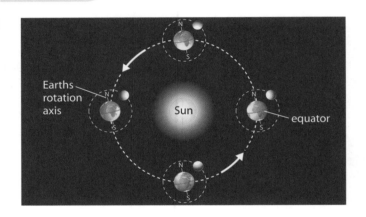

What else do we know about the orbit?

The Earth rushes around the Sun at 108,000 km per hour. This is very fast, but you don't feel it moving.

It takes $365\frac{1}{4}$ days to make one orbit. Although this is only a little more than a year, it would gradually cause the seasons to end up at the wrong time.

So every four years we add the four $\frac{1}{4}$ days together and add an extra day onto the year. This is called a 'leap' year. It has 366 days with 29 days in February.

Year

The time it takes for the Earth to make a single orbit of the Sun.

Pope Gregory XIII (1582)

Defined the rule that a leap day would occur in any year divisible by 4.

 **On track**

1   Mr Hills wants his class to model the Earth, Sun and Moon.
    He gives them some objects they can do this with.

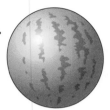

   (a) Write Earth, Moon and Sun in the table below to
       show what each object should model.

Melon	Marble	Poppy Seed

   (b) How can the class move the objects to model what causes a year?
       Choose the correct statement.

   - spin the Earth on its axis
   - spin the Sun on its axis
   - move the Earth around the Sun
   - move the Sun around the Earth

 Aiming higher

2   Mr Hills gave his class a short quiz.

1 The number of days it takes for the Earth to orbit the Sun.	1	7	24	28	$365\frac{1}{4}$
2 How many times the Earth spins on its axis in one day.	1	7	24	28	$365\frac{1}{4}$
3 The number of times the Earth spins on its axis in one year.	1	7	24	28	$365\frac{1}{4}$
4 The number of hours it takes for the Earth to spin once on its axis.	1	7	24	28	$365\frac{1}{4}$

   (a) Copy the quiz. Circle the correct answers.

3   The years 2008, 2012 and 2016 are all leap years. They are all divisible by four. They
    all have an extra day, 29th February.

   (a) Explain why a leap year is longer than every other year.

   (b) Which of these years will be leap years?   **2027   2020   2023   2032**

 How well am I doing?

On track

I can explain what the Earth's orbit looks like.

Aiming higher

I can explain what a leap year is.

20 How does the Moon move?

- The Moon orbits the Earth about once a month.
- The shape of the Moon appears to change as it goes around the orbit.

If there is a clear sky, watch out for the Moon tonight. How much of it will be lit up?
Is it bigger or smaller than last night? Do you know when there will next be a full Moon?
As the Moon orbits the Earth, we see different amounts of the Moon lit by the Sun.
These are called the phases of the moon.

How often does the Moon orbit the Earth?

The word 'month' comes from the word 'Moon', because it takes about a month for it to go around once.

How does the Moon look at different times of the month?

A full Moon (Wed 9th): The Moon at the first point in its orbit. The sun is shining straight onto the face of the Moon.

A new Moon (Wed 23rd): The Moon is now halfway round its orbit. The Sun is more or less behind it so it looks dark.

Sun	Mon	Tue	Wed	Thur	Fri	Sat
		1	2	3	4	5
6	7	8	9	10	11	12
13	14	15	16	17	18	19
20	21	22	23	24	25	26
27	28	29	30	31		

A waning Moon (Wed 16th): The Moon has gone a quarter of the way round the Earth. Sunshine hits it from the left-hand side.

A waxing half Moon (Wed 30th): When the Moon is three-quarters of the way around its orbit. The sunshine is lighting it from the right-hand side.

Gibbous Moon

When more than one half of the Moon is bright, but it is not completely lit up.

Crescent Moon

When less than half of the Moon is bright, but it is not completely dark.

On track

1 This calendar shows the phases of the Moon over three months. On the 11th October there was a new Moon.

Spot the pattern and then answer the questions.

	October					November					December				
Mon	2	9	16	23	30		6	13	20	27		4	11	18	25
Tue	3	10	17	24	31		7	14	21	28		5	12	19	26
Wed	4	11 ●	18	25 ○		1	8	15	22	29		6	13	20	27
Thur	5	12	19	26		2	9 ●	16	23 ○	30		7	14	21	28
Fri	6	13	20	27		3	10	17	24		1	8 ●	15	22 ○	29
Sat	7	14	21	28		4	11	18	25		2	9	16	23	30
Sun	1	8	15	22	29	5	12	19	26		3	10	17	24	31

Key ● = New Moon   ○ = Full Moon

(a) On what dates was there a full Moon?

(b) Give two dates in December when the Moon was half lit up.

(c) How many orbits of the Earth did the Moon make between 11th October and 8th December?

Aiming higher

2 This diagram shows the Moon making one complete orbit of the Earth.

(a) How long does it take the Moon to go through one complete cycle of its phases?

(b) Explain the difference between a gibbous and a crescent Moon.

(c) What do the words 'waxing' and 'waning' mean when we are talking about the appearance of the moon?

(d) Explain why a full moon is bright and a new moon is dark.

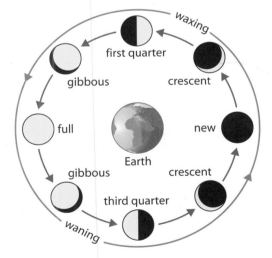

How well am I doing?

On track

I can state how long it takes for the Moon to make one complete orbit of the Earth.

Aiming higher

I can explain why the appearance of the Moon changes over a month.

21 What causes day and night?

- Day and night is caused by the Earth spinning on its axis.
- At any moment the time is different at different places on Earth.

When our part of the Earth faces the Sun, it is day. It will be night for us when our part of the Earth does not face the Sun. When it is daytime for us, it is night on the opposite side of the Earth. All times are compared with the time in Greenwich, London. As you move further east or west, the time of day changes to keep in step with the position of the Earth relative to the Sun.

How did Leopard class use a model to explain day and night?

Sian has a torch to represent the Sun. It does not move. Luke has a globe with a figure at the top. He takes care to hold it so that it is tilted, just like the Earth is. He turns it slowly. The torch shines on the globe. They see if the figure is lit up or in the dark.

The figure is facing the Sun: It is day.

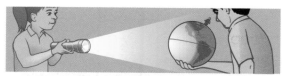

The figure faces away from the Sun: It is night.

Sian said, 'The Sun stays still. Night and day happen because the Earth spins.

'I wonder why the number of hours of day and night aren't always the same.'

Luke said, 'The Earth must spin on its axis once every 24 hours – once a day.

'That's because the earth is tilted so in summer the northern hemisphere gets more sun than the southern hemisphere.'

What time is it on different parts of the Earth?

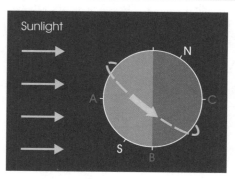

Sunlight

Noon: People standing at point A are directly facing the Sun. For them it is the middle of the day. It is 12 a.m.

Sunset: People standing at point B see the Sun setting in the sky. It is turning from night into day.

Midnight: People standing at point C cannot see the Sun at all. It is dark and the time is 12 p.m.

Points A, B and C are at different places and the time is different too.

Earth's axis

An imaginary line going through the Earth's centre from north to south.

Greenwich Mean Time (GMT)

The time compared with that in Greenwich, London.

On track

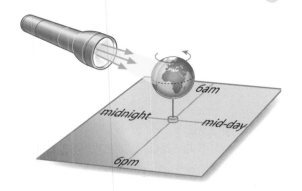

1   Mr Hills gave his class a worksheet on how to build a model that might show them what causes night and day.

   (a) What are they using to represent the Sun and the Earth?

   (b) Do they keep the torch still or move it around?

   (c) Do they keep the globe still or move it around?

   (d) Explain how they might use this model to explain day and night.

   (e) What does one turn of the globe represent?

Aiming higher

2   The time in London is mid-day: 12 noon. This table shows the time in some other parts of the world compared with London.

← ← WEST ← ←				→ → EAST → →	
Place	Mexico	Falkland Islands	London	Oman	Hong Kong	New Zealand
Time	4 am	8 am	12 noon	4 pm	8 pm	12 pm

   (a) Name the place that is 6 hours behind London.

   (b) What places are likely to be in daylight when it is noon in London?

   (c) Where is it likely to be night when it is noon in London?

   (d) Explain in your own words why the times are different.

How well am I doing?

On track

I can explain what causes night and day.

Aiming higher

I can tell you why the times in different places are different.

22 What was Ptolemy's big idea?

● The Earth was once thought to be at the centre of the Universe.

● Many famous scientists had ideas that Ptolemy used in this model.

Ptolemy was a famous Greek scientist who lived from 90 AD to 168 AD. He proposed a model of the solar system which was accepted as true until the Middle Ages. This model was changed when other scientists like Galileo and Copernicus made observations that didn't fit with Ptolemy's ideas.

What was Ptolemy's model of planets and stars?

Ptolemy had a **geocentric** view of the solar system. He thought that:

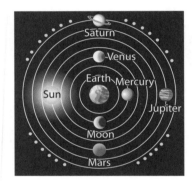

- The Earth is at the centre of the Universe.
- The Earth is stationary and does not move.
- Eight spheres surround the Earth.
- The spheres contain the Moon, Mercury, Venus, the Sun, Mars, Jupiter, Saturn, and the stars.
- They move in complicated patterns around the sky.

The theory was backed up by two key observations.

- As you look into the sky it appears that the stars, Sun, and planets move across the sky.
- The Earth is solid and you cannot feel it moving. Since it is still, other bodies must move around it.

Who else held this view?

Alhazen was a Muslim scientist who lived in Egypt. He wrote his book The *Model of the Motions of Each of the Seven Planets* in about 1038 AD.

He said, 'The earth as a whole is a round sphere whose centre is the centre of the world. It is stationary in its [the world's] middle, fixed in it and not moving in any direction nor moving with any of the varieties of motion, but always at rest.'

He was the first person to use mathematics to describe the motions of the planets.

Geocentric	Celestial
Having the Earth as a centre of our solar system. 'Geo' means Earth.	Relating to the sky or heavens.

On track

1   Mr Hills gave his class some statements about what scientists now think our solar system looks like. He asked them to compare these with the ideas of Ptolemy.

What scientists now know	Was Ptolemy correct?
A The Sun is at the centre of our solar system	
B The Earth orbits the Sun	
C The Moon orbits the Earth	
D The Sun, Earth and Moon spin on their axis	
E The planets have elliptical orbits	
F Our solar system contains eight planets	
G The solar system is not at the centre of the Universe	
H The solar system also contains meteors, asteroids and comets	

(a) Copy out the table. Complete the second column by writing 'He was right', 'He was wrong' or 'He didn't mention it' to show if Ptolemy agreed or disagreed with the views of modern scientists.

(b) Explain in your own words what the main difference was between Ptolemy's idea and the modern one.

Aiming higher

2   Leopard class researched some other early scientists. They each had an important idea about the Earth, planets and stars.

Scientist	Date	Country	Big idea
Anaximenes	560 BC	Greek	Stars are fixed inside a sphere
Pythagoras	550 BC	Greek	The Earth is a star
Aristarchus	300 BC	Greek	The Sun is the centre of the solar system
Aryabhata	499 AD	Indian	The Earth spins once a day

(a) How did each scientist agree or disagree with what we know now?

(b) Make a timeline to show these scientists and Ptolemy.

How well am I doing?

On track

I can describe the geocentric model of the Universe.

Aiming higher

I can tell you about some famous scientists who developed this model.

23 What was Copernicus's big idea?

- Copernicus did not agree with the geocentric model.
- **Galileo used a telescope to prove Copernicus's model was a good one.**

Nicolas Copernicus lived in the Russian province of Poland from 1473 to 1543. He set out his **heliocentric** view of the Universe, which put the **Sun** at its centre rather than the Earth. His ideas caused great controversy. They clashed with views that had been held for centuries and with the views of the Catholic Church.

What was Copernicus's model of planets and stars?

Copernicus based his heliocentric model on his observation of the movements of the Earth, Moon and other planets. He found if he put the Sun at the centre of the solar system he could explain their movements much better than Ptolemy had.

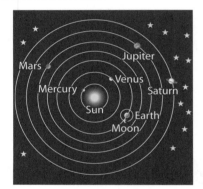

His main ideas were that:
- The Earth is one of seven planets circling a stationary Sun.
- The Earth moves in three ways: it rotates every day, moves around the Sun once a year, and tilts on its axis.
- The apparent movements of the Sun, stars and other planets can be explained by the movements of the Earth.

How did Galileo improve the model?

Galileo was one of the first people to use a telescope. This let him observe the skies in more detail and he became a champion of the heliocentric model.

Heliocentric
Having the Sun as a centre of the universe. 'Helio' means sun.

Proof
Evidence that is good enough to say an idea is true.

On track

1   Mr Hills gave his class some statements about what scientists now think our solar system looks like. He asked them to compare these with the ideas of Copernicus.

What scientists now know	Was Copernicus correct?
A The Sun is at the centre of our solar system	
B The Earth orbits the Sun	
C The Moon orbits the Earth	
D The Sun, Earth and Moon spin on their axis	
E The planets have elliptical orbits	
F Our solar system contains eight planets	
G The solar system is not at the centre of the Universe	
H The solar system also contains meteors, asteroids and comets	

(a) Copy out the table. Complete the second column by writing 'He was right', 'He was wrong' or 'He didn't mention it' to show if Copernicus agreed or disagreed with the views of modern scientists.

(b) Explain in your own words what the main difference was between Copernicus's idea and the modern one.

Aiming higher

2   Leopard class researched some more early scientists.

Scientist	Date	Country	Big idea
Galileo	1632	Italian	Published evidence to support Copernicus
Najm al-Dīn al-Qazwīnī al-Kītibī	1277 AD	Arabic	Suggested heliocentric model, but changed his mind later on.
Nilakantha Somayaji	1500 AD	Indian	Planets orbit the Sun; Sun orbits the Earth.
Tycho Brahe	1587 AD	Danish	Planets orbit the Sun; Sun and Moon orbits the Earth.

(a) How did each scientist agree or disagree with what we know now?

(b) How do you think scientists get their ideas about the solar system and the universe?

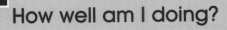

How well am I doing?

On track

I can describe the heliocentric model of the Universe.

Aiming higher

I can name some famous scientists who developed this model.

24 Is the Earth flat or spherical?

- People from many cultures used to think that the Earth was flat.
- There is convincing evidence to show the Earth is almost spherical.

The ancient Greeks thought that the Earth was flat. To them this made sense. After all, if you climbed a mountain you could see the Earth below was flat. No matter how far you walked, it was still flat. Today nearly everyone is convinced that the Earth is spherical.

Why did people think the Earth was flat?

Around 400 or 500 BC the Greek thinker Herodotus drew his view of the Earth. The Earth was flat and surrounded by water.

In ancient India the view was that 'the Earth is a disc that consists of four continents grouped around the central mountain Meru like the petals of a flower'.

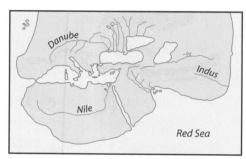

World map of Herodotus

What is the evidence for the Earth being spherical?

These facts help show that the Earth is spherical.

- At sea you see high mountains before low ground because the Earth curves.
- When ships disappear over the horizon, the bottom of the ship disappears first, before the top. If the Earth was flat, it would just get smaller and smaller.
- It is possible to go completely around the Earth and return to where you started.
- An artificial satellite can circle the Earth continuously.
- The Earth appears as a sphere on photographs from space no matter where you take them.

The spherical Earth

Evidence

Facts that support a particular view.

Norse people

People from Scandinavia.

On track

1   On 12 April 1961 the Soviet cosmonaut Yuri Gagarin became the first person to see the Earth from space.

   (a) Would he have said that the Earth was flat or spherical?

   (b) What evidence would he have used to convince you of his view?

2   Use the Internet to research what the Earth looks like from space. Explain why this supports the spherical view of the Earth.

3   Draw a picture of what the ancient Indian people thought the Earth looked like.

4   Find out how the ancient Norse and Japanese people described the shape of Earth.

Aiming higher

5   Leopard class looked at this picture. Some were asked to believe in a flat Earth, others a spherical Earth.

   (a) What arguments would the Flat Earth group use with the picture to justify their view of the world?

   (b) What arguments would the Spherical Earth group use with the picture to justify their view of the world?

How well am I doing?

On track

I know how ancient cultures described their flat Earth.

Aiming higher

I can give you evidence to support the view that the Earth is spherical.

25 What was Sir Isaac Newton's big idea?

- At the age of 23 Isaac Newton realised that gravity is a force.
- Scientists are still finding out about what causes gravity to this day.

Isaac Newton was born on Christmas day 1642. Earlier that year, the great Italian astronomer-scientist Galileo had died. It is said that Newton realised the force of gravity existed when an apple fell from a tree and hit him on the head. Gravity is why the apple fell down instead of up, and why people don't float in the air.

What did Galileo discover?

Galileo discovered that everything falls at the same speed. At the time everyone thought this was a silly idea and that heavy things would fall fastest. You might find this hard to believe because air gets in the way and slows falling things down. Galileo used the scientific method to prove this was wrong.

He dropped two round balls off the Leaning Tower of Pisa. One was heavy and one was light. His test showed that both hit the ground at the same time. But he didn't know why!

How did Isaac Newton improve the theory?

Like Galileo, Newton thought that mathematics could explain how the universe works. He developed Galileo's ideas and used mathematics to prove his theories. He was able to explain how objects move on Earth and in space. His theory was revolutionary.

Newton understood that gravity is the force of attraction between two objects. All objects have gravity. Exactly how much depends on the size of the object. The larger the object, the bigger the pull of gravity. A large object like the Earth pulls objects toward it very well.

Pisa

A university city in Italy with a famous leaning tower.

Woolsthorpe, Lincolnshire

Newton's birthplace and location of his famous apple tree.

On track

1   Sir Isaac Newton thought that a force must cause an apple to drop from a tree.

   (a) Which of these forces causes the apple to fall?

a pulling force from the tree	a pushing force from the apple
a pulling force from the Earth	a pushing force from the air

   (b) What name do we give to this force?

Aiming higher

2   Mr Hills said that ideas about gravity are continually changing.

Scientist	Date	Big idea
Abū Rayhān al-Bīrūnī	1000s	Proposed gravity exists between stars and planets
Alhazen	1000s	Proposed that heavenly bodies follow the laws of physics
Galileo and Newton	1600s	Developed the ideas of gravity by using mathematics
Albert Einstein	1905	Developed his special theory of gravity, which explained how gravity works.
Stephen Hawking	2010	Said that the universe was created by gravity

   (a) Draw a timeline of these scientists with their major ideas.

   (b) Use the Internet to add a few more.

How well am I doing?

On track

I can tell you how the theory of gravity first came about.

Aiming higher

I can draw a timeline showing how the theory of gravity has developed.

26 What is weight?

- A force called gravity pulls objects towards the centre of the Earth.
- Weight is the way scientists measure the force of gravity.

Imagine holding up an apple. You have to keep pushing it upwards or it will fall. The force of gravity is pulling it down. This force is also called **weight**. Weight is measured in units called Newtons (N). The force pulling down on one apple is about 1 Newton.

Which way does gravity pull?

Gravity is pulling the Earth and the apple towards each other.

The Earth is a ball, so 'down' is towards the middle of the Earth. Gravity pulls all objects towards the middle of the Earth.

Everything on Earth has weight. Weight is the name given to how much something is pulled down by gravity.

The weight of objects varies on the Earth. You would be about 3 newtons heavier at the North Pole and about 1 newton lighter up a tall mountain. At the centre of the Earth you would weigh nothing because you would be pulled equally in all directions.

Why can astronauts jump so high?

You would get a surprise if you weighed yourself on the Moon. You would weigh much less than you do on Earth. Instead of weighing about 180 Newtons, you would weigh about 30 Newtons. No wonder astronauts can jump so high!

The Moon is smaller than the Earth, so its pull of gravity is less.

Remember that the amount of gravity depends on the size of the object. It is not because there is no air on the Moon.

Force

A push or a pull. Forces make things move. They can also stop things moving.

Gravity

The force that pulls objects towards the centre of the Earth.

On track

1 Barney the dog jumps up to catch a stick.

  (a) What force pulls Barney back to the ground?

  (b) Which would be the correct arrow to add to the picture above to show the direction of that force?

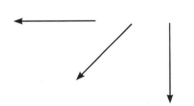

Aiming higher

2 This astronaut is jumping on the surface of the Moon.

  (a) How would the lower gravity change the height he could jump up to?

  (b) What difference does the low gravity make to his weight?

  (c) What would the astronaut notice about how fast he falls?

  (d) Why is the pull of gravity less on the Moon than on the Earth?

How well am I doing?

On track

I know that the force of gravity pulls objects downwards towards the centre of the Earth.

Aiming higher

I know that weight is the pull of gravity due to the pull of the Earth.

27 What effect can drag forces have?

- Air resistance is a drag force that slows things down.
- **Water resistance is another drag force that slows things down.**

Have you noticed that when you ride your bike the air seems to slow you down? A similar thing happens when you swim though the water. The forces stopping you moving are called air and water resistance. They are drag forces and depend on the shape, size and speed of the object that is moving through the air or water.

What effect does air resistance have?

Air resistance is a drag force. It slows things down that move through air. If there were no air, then an object would just keep moving and not slow down.

The streamlined shape helps to reduce the drag force.

The parachute's large canopy increases the drag and slows the parachute down.

What effect does water resistance have?

Water resistance is also a drag force. It slows things down that move through water.

The streamlined shape of submarines help to reduce water resistance.

Drag

To pull with a force.

Streamlined

A shape that offers the least air or water resistance. Air or water flow over some shapes better than others.

On track

1   Leopard class had to drop four pieces of plasticine into a cylinder of thin wallpaper paste. They timed how long it took for each one to fall.

	Shape 1	Shape 2	Shape 3	Shape 4
Time it took to fall	0.55 s	1.0 s	1.5 s	2.5 s

(a) Explain what they would have to do to make their investigation fair.

(b) Savita predicted, 'The most streamlined shape falls the quickest.' Was she right?

Aiming higher

2   Leopard class made four parachutes from squares of polythene of different sizes. These had the same mass attached and were dropped from the same height. They measured how long it took for the parachutes to fall from the same height.

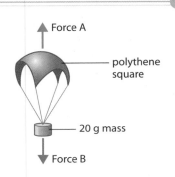

Force A

polythene square

20 g mass

Force B

(a) What is the name of the downward force B?

(b) What is the name of the upward force A?

(c) What did they keep the same, change and measure in their investigation? Put your answers in a table.

Area of parachute (cm³)	Time to fall (s)
9	3.4
16	4.8
25	7.0
36	10.6

(d) Describe the pattern in their results table between the area of the parachute and the time taken for it to fall to the ground.

(e) Plot a line graph of their results.

(f) Use it to predict how long it would take a parachute that had an area of 20 cm³ to fall.

How well am I doing?

On track

I can explain what air and water resistance do.

Aiming higher

I can explain how the shape of an object affects its air or water resistance.

28 What causes friction?

- Friction is a force that happens when two materials rub against each other.
- Both high and low friction can be useful.

Most forces 'get things going', but friction slows things down or stops them. This drag force is caused by two surfaces rubbing together. Friction is higher when the surfaces are dry and rough, and lower when they are smooth and wet. Friction also causes heat. Sometimes high friction can be a good thing. At other times it can cause problems.

How can friction be useful?

Having lots of friction between two surfaces can be very useful!

The brakes rub on the wheel rim. High friction between them slows the bike down.

The treads on the tyres cause lots of friction when they rub against the road. This gives lots of grip.

Trainers have rough, rubber soles. High friction between them and the path stops you slipping.

How can friction be reduced?

There is less friction if the surfaces are smooth or a lubricant is used.

There is little friction here because the ice is smooth.

The engine oil lubricates the engine. The smooth liquid reduces friction.

The water on these chutes helps reduce friction and acts as a lubricant.

Friction
A force that slows or stops movement.

Lubricant
A substance that reduces friction such as oil or grease.

On track

1   Leopard class investigated the question
'What kind of surfaces cause the least
friction?' They decided to pull a trainer
over different surfaces using a Newton
meter. At first the trainer did not move.
As they increased the pull, the trainer
started to move. They measured the
force on the Newton meter.

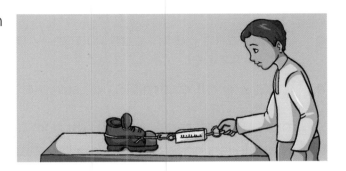

(a) What forces are acting on the trainer to make it move and stop it moving?

(b) What name is given to the force caused by the surfaces rubbing?

(c) Which of these pieces of equipment would they need for their investigation?

trainer	tape measure	Newton meter	table
thermometer	surfaces to test	beaker	stopwatch

(d) What MUST they keep the same, change and measure in their investigation?
Put your answer in a neat table.

Aiming higher

2   Here are the results of their
investigation.

(a) Which materials produced the
most and **least** friction?

(b) Which TWO materials produced
the same amount of friction?

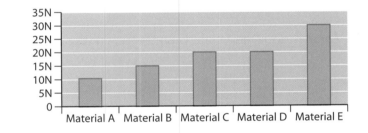

(c) Which material does the trainer slide over most easily?

(d) Draw what you think the surfaces of most and least friction look like.

3   Explain the following:

(a) Walking on wet ice is difficult.

(b) Scouts light fires by rubbing two sticks together.

(c) Sliding down a rope can burn your hands.

How well am I doing?

On track

I can explain what causes friction and say if
it is useful or not.

Aiming higher

I can explain how to test for friction.

29 What can levers and gears do?

- Levers and gears can magnify a force or make something move further.

- **They are all examples of simple machines that make our lives easier.**

You might use a screwdriver to open a tin of paint or a pair of scissors to cut some paper. Both these levers have a pivot. Your bike has gears to make it easier to change speed, and a hand whisk moves quickly because of its gears.

What can levers do?

Levers are simple machines that change the direction or magnify a force. They have something rigid that moves on a pivot. Good examples are crowbars, scissors, and bottle openers.

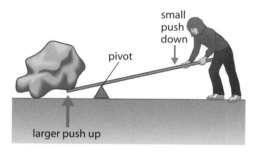

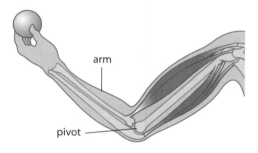

Force magnifier: A small push down with your hand can push up the heavy rock with a big force.

Distance magnifier: A small movement of your arm muscle brings about a big movement of your hand.

What can gears do?

Gears are wheels with teeth that fit together. When one moves, the other moves in the opposite direction. Good examples are pendulum clocks, some toys and washing machines.

Force magnifier: A small force turns the small gear. The larger gear turns more slowly but with a larger force. This is used in hand whisks and bicycles.

Distance magnifier: The large gear turns slowly. It makes the small gear move quicker and move further. This makes cars go faster on flat roads.

Magnify

To make bigger.

Pivot

The point about which something turns.

On track

1   Scissors, fishing rods and wheelbarrows are all examples of levers. They all have a pivot, and somewhere they receive a push or a pull.

The scissors cut the strong string.

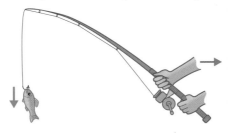

Turning the rod lifts the fish.

The wheelbarrow can lift a heavy load.

   (a) Draw each of these levers. Label where the pivot (turning point) is in each.

   (b) Which ONE of these is a distance magnifier? Explain your answer.

   (c) Which TWO are force magnifiers? Explain your answer.

Aiming higher

2   These drawings show the high and low gears on a bike. The larger gear connected to the pedal pulls the smaller wheel gear with a chain.

high gear speed

low gear speed

	Number of cogs in the gear	
	Pedal cog	Wheel cog
High gear	40	10
Low gear	40	20

   (a) How many turns does the wheel cog make for every turn of the pedal gear when in **high** gear?

   (b) How many turns does the wheel cog make for every turn of the pedal gear when in **low** gear?

   (c) Are the bike's gears a force or distance magnifier? Explain this.

   (d) Do the pedal and wheel cogs move in the same or the opposite direction?

How well am I doing?

On track

I can explain why levers and gears are useful.

Aiming higher

I can explain how levers and gears act as force and distance magnifiers.

Index